"It is Mum's birthday on Thursday,"
said Biff. "What shall we get her as
a surprise?"

"This perfume smells like Mum,"
said Chip. "It's called 'Fern' but
it's thirty pounds."

Biff looked in her purse. All she had
was seven pounds. Chip and Kipper
had five pounds <u>ea</u>ch.

"All we have is seventeen pounds,"
said Chip. "We still need thirteen pounds."

"How can we get it for her?" said Biff.
"Let's ask Dad what we should do."

Just then there was a whoosh and
a bang. A firework burst up in the sky.

6

"What on earth was that?" asked Dad.
Then, more fireworks went off.

It was Uncle Max. He was the person
letting off the fireworks.

"He is so crazy," said Dad.
"He never l<u>ea</u>rns."
The children loved Uncle Max.

"May I stay for a day or two?"
asked Uncle Max. "I'll be away
by Thursday."

"Did you say Thursday?" said Dad.
"I certainly did," said Uncle Max.
"I'm a person to keep his word."

11

The children had fun with Uncle Max.
They made a birthday cake for Mum.
It had purple icing.

"You have been all over the world,"
said Kipper. "Tell us a story, Uncle Max."

"I was diving for pearls when a giant
turtle swam by. The turtle wanted me
to swim with it," said Uncle Max.

"The turtle took me to the sea bed. There
I saw a shell with a huge pearl inside."

"But an octopus took a firm grip on my leg. I pulled and pulled but I could not get free.

It was my worst moment ever! Just then
I heard a girl singing. I was amazed!"

"She was a mermaid. She took a firm hold of my hand and pulled me away from the octopus."

"Uncle Max!" said Kipper. "There are
no such things as mermaids."

The children put on a concert. They
sang songs and performed a
little play.

Uncle Max loved the concert. He gave them all some pocket money.

So, the children could get Mum her
favourite perfume for her birthday,
after all.

Uncle Max gave Mum a box.
"What can it be?" asked Mum.

Inside was a big pearl for Mum.
"It's thanks to a mermaid," said Uncle Max.